. . . and a time to dance

. . . and a time to dance

by NORMA CANNER

photography by HARRIET KLEBANOFF

plays, inc.   boston
Publishers

to Leonard and to Lewis

acknowledgments

WE WOULD like to thank the many people in the Massachusetts Department of Mental Health who recognized the value of and who encouraged the use of creative movement in the Community Clinical Nursery Schools — Dr. B.R. Hutcheson, Dr. Lewis Klebanoff, Dorothy Tucker, and Barbara Jean Seabury. We want to express our deep appreciation to the teachers for their enthusiasm and cooperation.

To the children and their parents, a mere "thank you" will never be enough. They have taught us so much — about expectations, creativity, beauty, and about sorrow and joy. If this book in any way helps to demonstrate some of what we have felt and learned, it will in a small way repay our debt to them. We came to teach, and we stayed to learn.

Norma Canner
Harriet Klebanoff

preface to the second edition

ACROSS the country and everywhere I go, teachers express increasing interest and desire to learn how to use creative movement in the classroom. Public schools are starting to hire dance specialists, not only to teach children — normal and handicapped, exceptional and gifted — but to give the teaching staff in-service training so that dance and movement can be an integral part of the school curriculum, in physical education classes and in the classroom.

In colleges and universities and teacher training institutions, dance and movement courses are flourishing, as more and more young people seem to understand the importance of dance in a society where it is often so hard to keep the psychic and the physical self in balance.

Because of this fast-growing interest in educational dance in the United States, it seemed important to me and to the publishers that this book, originally published several years ago, be reissued so that it would be available for use by specialists, physical education and regular classroom teachers. The creative movement techniques described in the book were developed in the course of my work as teacher-consultant for six years in a preschool program for retarded children.

Experts in early childhood education are seriously examining the place of dance in relation to children's early awareness of their bodies and of movement as a means of expressing their emotions and growing awareness of self. Mastering the techniques of body control and the meaning and possibilities of body movement enables children to gain the self-confidence necessary to other areas of learning.

Norma Canner

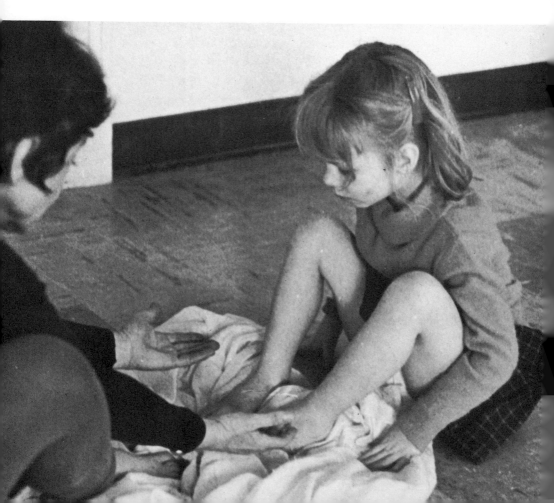

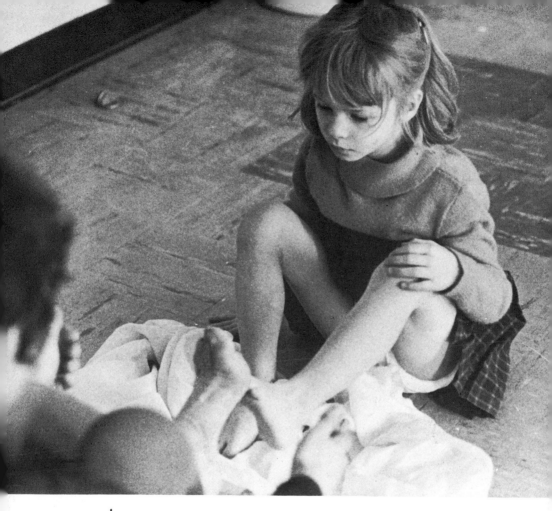

introduction

I USED TO THINK that only special people had talent and only special people had the need to express their creative feelings. I didn't know that anyone could dance, that people of great differences could communicate through movement, sharing their joys and pleasures, their angers and frustrations. Nor did I know that a large group of people could dance together and feel as one, or that you could dance alone and still be a part of a group.

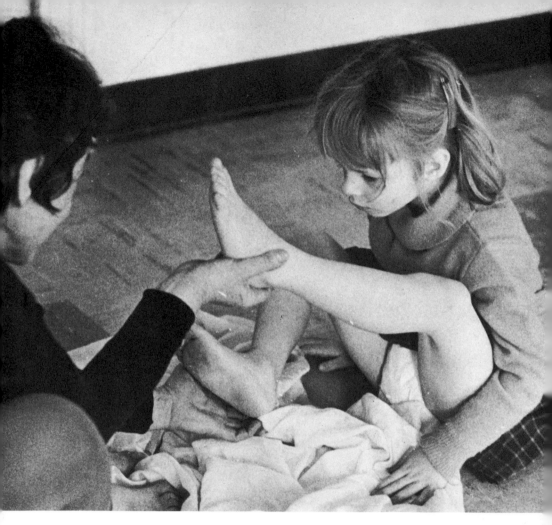

Many years ago I met Miss Barbara Mettler, teacher of Modern Dance, who showed me new ways of seeing, thinking, and feeling. She taught me the joy of dancing with others and the exciting potential of improvisation. Most important of all, I learned that each human being has something to say, that it is up to the teacher to provide an atmosphere where people can feel free to express themselves. I found that I was able to work with and teach people who had a variety of physical and mental differences. After all, most of us have a handicap of some sort and it is only by degrees that we vary or differ. I learned to use and understand the nature of basic dance and was able when confronted with new problems to develop and use creative movement to meet the needs of these new situations.

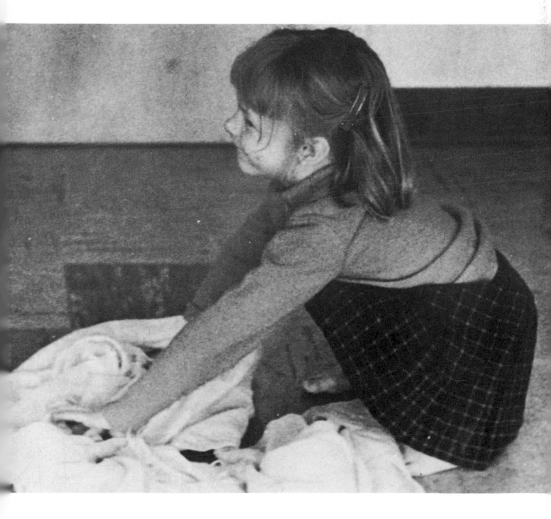

And so it began to happen with increasing regularity that dance workshops and lecture demonstrations would provoke requests for classes: for children with cerebral palsy, for children who were emotionally disturbed, for the retarded, for mentally ill adults and teenagers, for Headstart children and teachers, for college students of child development and their supervisors. They all seemed to find something of value in this experience with creative movement. Many of these people and groups had special problems so that I had to adapt myself and the material to suit and meet the needs of the people in these different groups. From the first, the successes were greater than the failures. This was an area where everyone could experience some success and satisfaction, both physical and emotional, where they could feel part of a whole. Formerly the pattern of failure

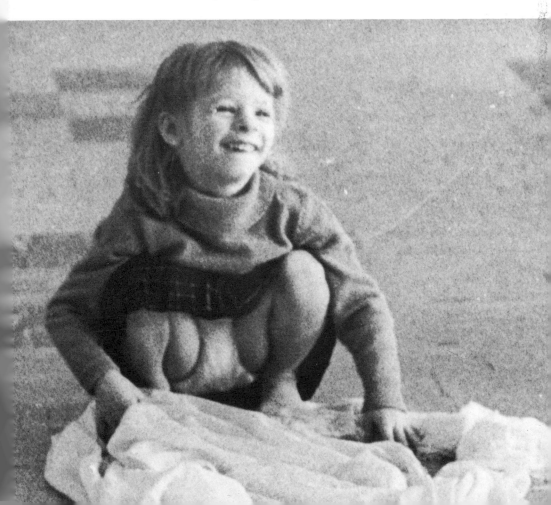

had been in many of these lives too familiar, resulting in feelings of frustration and isolation.

For the last six years I have been a teacher consultant for the Massachusetts Department of Mental Health, in the Preschool Program for Retarded Children. These are the children pictured in this book. They have taught me as much as I have them.

For the young child, movement is a way of exploring and discovering his world and himself. As an infant he moves indiscriminately. He soon discovers and then learns to control his body. He uses his body to move about and explore first his immediate environment and then a broader world. At points in his development he discovers his arms, his legs, his eyes and ears, and soon realizes that these are part of him. His self image is formed in part by these discoveries of and about his moving body. His body is his basic tool for dealing with his world before he learns to verbalize and intellectualize his thoughts and feelings.

As the child matures the pressures of society tend to repress his free body movement. The child must learn to control his need to move when it is time to be still, to control even his joy so that it fits with society's acceptable ways of expressing joy. Because these controls may be necessary in our highly complicated world, it becomes even more important that the child retain some outlets through which he can express what he feels and that he can find a satisfying way to create something unique and know the pleasure of involvement. Art and

music have long been recognized as excellent media for the child's self-expression and creativity. In art the child uses images, in music he uses sound, in creative movement he uses his entire body to communicate, to create, and to express. Movement is very much a part of the language of the young child.

What is creative movement? In this instance it is dancing with young children, providing them with an opportunity to explore and discover their bodies, their feelings, and the textures, shapes, and sounds around them, alone or in a group. It is an environment in which the shy child can lose his inhibitions when intrigued by strange, exciting instruments and materials. It is an environment in which the aggressive child is given an outlet for pent-up energies or hostile feelings. It is when every child is offered a time to experience the joy and freedom of using his body and his creative uniqueness . . . a time to dance.

Perhaps the most important reason I believe that creative movement should be part of a child's life is that unlike many other activities in which children participate there is no right or wrong way to express or to discover. There is no failure. All that is required of a child is that he be involved.

While he is learning more about himself, he realizes that he can now use his arms, legs, eyes, and ears to discover a room, the sounds in a room, the child next to him, the textures of materials, the space in which he moves, and the rhythms he can make.

Music as composed by others can regiment or dictate the mood and time pattern. Using the children's own rhythmic feelings and movements increases their sense of acceptance and self-worth. When a child beats a rhythm for others to follow, he is aware that he is the leader, he can decide when the group will dance, and when it will stop, if the sound quality will be loud or soft, or the time fast or slow. When he plays for the teacher alone— it is a duet—between them, a rare and unusual dialogue. They are equal, responding to each other on a level that rarely happens between a child and an adult. For music and sound accompaniments, the children have themselves, their hands and feet, their fingers and toes, their tongues and voices; there are all kinds of instruments—drums, bells, sticks, shakers, the sounds in the room, and the world around them. All this and more can make music for their dances.

Children vary in the advantages and disadvantages with which they are born, but they are all the same because they are children and they all have the same needs. That is why I like to dance with children and their teachers.

It is important that a teacher learn to feel movement, to develop her kinesthetic and visual senses. Her awareness can encourage the children's movement processes. She is the guide and most often the leader. She can expand and give structure to the dance experience. The teacher can reinforce learning by emphasizing the movements with her voice and words. She must be able to see when a child offers original movements, and accept his ideas. Inspiration will come from the children if she will only look.

Since it is up to the teacher to recognize and see with understanding eyes and heart the disposition and needs of her children, it seems only natural that the teacher becomes involved in movement exploration. Her participation will add another tool for gaining deeper insights into the understanding of children.

This book came about as a result of the many teachers I have met working with young children who wanted to know more about creative movement. They wanted specific material which would help them use this as a part of the class program.

In the pages ahead you will see and read about a typical class. The pictures were taken

over a year's time and represent a certain amount of growth, both physical and emotional. These pictures are an inspiration. The text is intended as a stimulus and a guide to help the teacher. However, she should not feel limited by what she sees and reads any more than she would limit the creative experience of the children. She can expand, develop, and adapt any and all of this material. It must suit her and the children's needs. The most important ingredient for a successful dance experience is enjoyment.

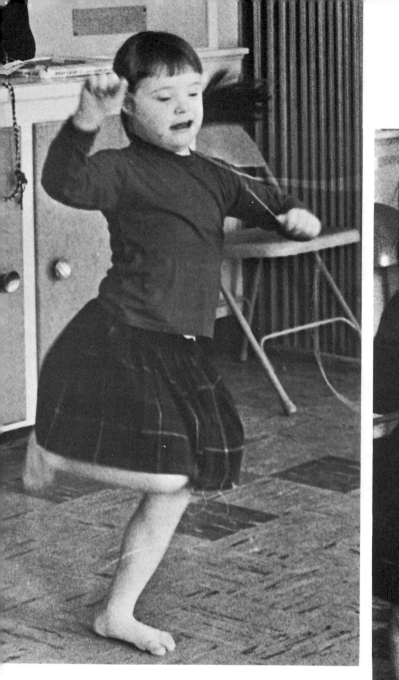

... and a time to dance

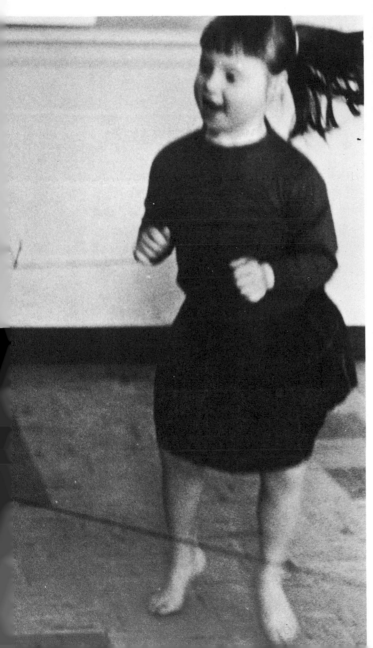

THE CREATIVE MOVEMENT which has been graphically expressed in the preceding pictures can provide children with a better awareness of themselves and the various parts of their bodies, with a nonverbal means of communicating, and with an increasing perception of the world around them. As you have seen, it includes body dynamics, dance, and all forms of free spontaneous movement.

The aims of a continuing program of creative movement are:

to allow the child sufficient freedom to express himself

to promote the growth of a healthy personality by encouraging awareness of the whole self through body action, by helping the child feel good about himself, by helping him become a member of a group

to foster self-respect and respect for the individuality of others

to help develop social awareness, the ability to make contact with another person and to sustain this relationship

to resolve conflict and hostility by channeling it constructively into body action and dance

to foster and sensitize the child's sensory abilities, stimulating emotional, physical, and intellectual growth

to define and refine concepts

The teacher's positive attitudes, understanding, and enjoyment of creative movement are essential. The teacher should not attempt to teach the children anything as structured as dancing; rather, she should motivate and stimulate the children to move. Initially, this will be teacher-directed as she helps develop interest in creative movement, and as she demonstrates the dynamics of body motion. Ultimately, the sessions should become child-centered and child-directed, with guidance and support from the teacher. This approach will give greater depth to the teacher's awareness and understanding of the needs and nature of her class. She will have another tool to help her interpret the behavior of each child—individually and within the group.

Although the children are in a group, creative movement is initially a personal and individual experience, gradually developing into one-to-one relationships, which culminate in group experiences. Each child has the opportunity to be himself, to explore movement, to be accepted on the basis of participation rather than on a preconceived idea. In this way, each child is encouraged to respect himself and to find his place in the group. When children have the opportunity to explore the space around them, to learn what the separate parts of their bodies are and what they can do, and to feel themselves wholly involved in a creative group activity, their motor and sensory competencies will develop in an atmosphere which can bring success and good feelings.

HOW TO BEGIN

It is not always possible to have a large empty room for a class in creative movement; therefore, the teacher must learn to make the most of the space that exists. It is not even advisable in the beginning to have a very large area because children can feel overwhelmed by a room that is too large. Also, the teacher may feel more comfortable starting in a smaller space because she can feel contact physically, see the group—and the individual children. It will help her to begin the class.

Naturally, it is easier to work with a small group—let's say fifteen, rather than thirty, children. If the group is large and there is an assistant or co-teacher available, half the children can participate in another activity. But even with a small group, an assistant is always of great benefit by being an instant follower of the teacher and by being able to cope with children who may be experiencing difficulty in following or even in joining the group. After the teacher has had some experience in the medium, larger classes will be easier; but a small group will always give her more opportunity to observe and to help individual children.

Surely this is an ideal situation; there are many teachers who will never have a class with only fifteen children and who will never have an assistant. So a teacher should use any and all of this material in ways which will work for her in her situation. She must always remember that she is unique; no situation is ever the same; and only by trial and error will she discover the best way to begin—for *her, her children*, and *her classroom.*

The teacher sets the stage for creative movement sessions by dressing appropriately in slacks, leotards with a skirt, or other non-confining garments. Interest is immediately stimulated by the "ceremony" of removing shoes and socks. Bare feet encourage greater freedom and reduce the chance of the children hurting thmselves or each other. The teacher is barefoot first, and she talks about sensations she is experiencing and anticipating: "It's different to

have your feet on the floor. Mmm, feel the floor. See, I'm wiggling my toes. Oh, look at David's feet. Let's see if we can all move our feet as he is."

The teacher must provide a place to put shoes so that the children can see them and know they are "safe." The children must be reassured that they can retrieve their possessions whenever they want them.

The next step for the teachers and the children who want to participate is to form a circle. This is a basic and natural group form for children: they can see each other and a feeling of unity is created—movements can be seen and shared. It is a way for the child to explore space in relation to himself and the group.

Sometimes the children will be seated in chairs in a circle, as young children are likely to be when they are listening to a story, singing, or having circle time. As the teacher senses restlessness in the children and is ready to start a new activity, she can begin creative-movement experiences right there. She might see a child swinging his legs and suggest, "See what John is doing; let's all do it with him."

In the circle, the child can go around, up and down, in and out. The child, through the movements of his own body, sees where he is when he goes in and when he goes out—how it looks and how it feels.

The teacher should recognize the floor as a structural limit in creative movement; it is difficult sometimes with a very lively class to sustain the group or even to form a group, and the floor acts as an aid. It helps the children to come together and to feel the involvement of creating and experiencing movements with each other.

Early in the creative-movement program the circle and the floor are frequently used in combination. The children lie on their stomachs in the circle and look at each other. They hold

each other's hands. They touch feet. They lie on their backs, stretching or shaking their legs in the air. As the program evolves, the children will do more in the sitting, kneeling, and standing positions.

The children start to feel differently about themselves as they see and explore. They not only do the movements themselves, but they see how other people look doing them. They look, observe, and concentrate. It is an excellent

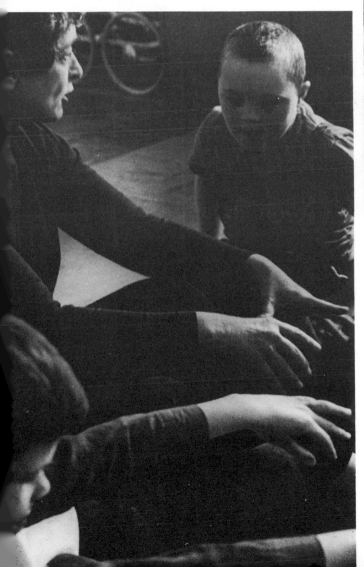

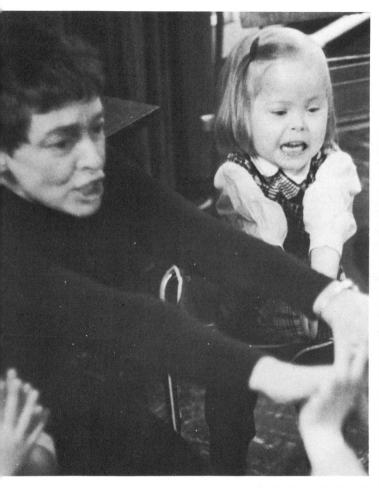

means of stimulating perceptual skills and developing large and small motor skills. At the same time, the teacher can reinforce the learning by emphasizing the movements with her voice and words. For example, she might say, "We go in . . . we go out." Or "Our hands are high . . . our hands are low."

Some children will not want to join the circle. The teacher should be aware of the child who pulls away or who waits outside the group. She can leave a place and let the child know that this space is being saved for him.

The children may want to break away from the circle, and, as one child leaves, others do, too. The teacher picks up the cue and encourages further movement by defining what the departing child or children are doing and by exaggerating with her own body actions what is happening.

Sometimes the teacher will not be able to form a circle with the children. They might start punching, pulling, or pushing. The teacher might pick up the punching and suggest to the whole group that it punch the air—"PUNCH, PUNCH!" Or it might be better to change the activity and to start another way. The class might need more energetic large-muscle activities, and the children can run, jump, or skip until some of their restlessness is gone and they can work better as a group. The teacher should accept any movement and in turn make it acceptable. She should help the children expend their energy until they have met their individual needs and are ready to relate to others.

The circle is "formally" re-established at appropriate times during the creative dance session. It may be a time for evaluation or planning; it may be a time to re-emphasize group feelings; it may be a time to introduce a new experience; it may be a time to change the mood of dance expression; it may be a time to look at each other again.

Because creative movement may be an entirely new experience, it is often necessary to shift rapidly from one area of concentration to another. For many reasons, the attention spans of the children can be short and interests limited. The time patterns become longer as the children become involved and do not need so much individual attention to be noticed or to be first.

Children who have experienced many failures tend to be afraid of involving themselves completely in situations that do not have a predetermined ending or result. They will need many kinds of support. Some children are embarrassed when it is suggested that they look at each other or that they touch each other; some giggle, shy away, or drop their eyes. When a child can tolerate the attention, the teacher should refer to him by name and support him through the experience with praise. Those who are made uncomfortable by this approach should be free to participate peripherally. The teacher will plan as well for the less actively involved as for the more involved by observing reactions to various stimuli and building on responses. The teacher must understand the fact that some children will not be able to accept the amount of freedom of expression inherent in creative movement; they will be disturbed by the possibilities of exposing feelings they want to conceal. For them the aims and techniques of creative movement can be emphasized in other parts of the class day (for example, exaggerating body movements in the physical handling of clay, dough, or paints) to help the child with other forms of self-expression. This child should participate when he decides he can.

THE ISOLATION OF SEPARATE PARTS
OF THE BODY

The isolation of separate body parts is one of
the most important steps in creative movement
and works well while the participants are in a
circle. Urging the children to become aware
of the separate parts of their bodies and what
these parts can do will prepare the children's
bodies for more imaginative exploration. If this
isolation is not accomplished, the possibilities
for new and creative movements are limited.
Monotony and sameness will result.

Therefore, a portion of each session should be spent in discovering movement possibilities. The children can see and explore the movements of a body part and its components.

The children feel differently about themselves as they see and explore. They learn that their shoulders can go up and down, forward and backward, and that they can create movements with their elbows. When a child wiggles his nose, the others may follow and begin to explore facial expressions. They discover the nose as part of the face, and as they wiggle and contort it, a variety of responses may be evoked—giggling, touching, or contemplating—but there is a common feeling of sharing, and this is good.

The children can be seated on the floor in a circle during this exploration of separate parts of the body. One of the children can lead the group by demonstrating a movement of the head or another part of the body until all the body parts have been explored. The teacher, of course, must use her judgment concerning how long the group is engaged in this activity. She can change or substitute any of this material so that it will be a successful experience. All the ways that separate parts of the body can be moved should be explored. For example:

Fingers and hands: Make circles with the thumbs; experiment with each finger—bending, separating, curling, stretching; experiment with movement of the fingers together—snapping, weaving in and out, making shapes and forms, tapping, making a fist, pounding, and slapping.

Arms: Movements with the arms can include pushing, pulling, stretching—up, down, into the circle; swinging—experimentally with one arm, moving slowly, then quickly, in straight lines, then in curved lines; experimenting with two arms together, making shapes, one arm up, one down. These movements can be done individually or in groups of two or more together. The teacher can give different children a chance to contribute a movement which the other children will follow.

Feet and legs: Different movements will result if the children are sitting or standing or lying on their backs or on their stomachs. Stamping, sliding, shuffling, scraping, tapping, and brushing can be done in a sitting or standing position; while on their backs they can wave their legs in the air—one up, one down; they can kick both legs up, separate the legs, then put them together. Ankles can be bent, toes can be wiggled, spread apart, stretched forward and back, and squeezed together.

Elbows: Touch elbows together, spread them apart, move forward and back; touch the knees; tap the elbows on the floor; make circles—one at a time, both together, forward and back.

Head: Bend the head forward, backward, sideward; shake it, roll it—in one direction and then in another.

Eyes: Open the eyes, shut them, blink them; look up, down, and side to side; rest; make circles.

Nose: Wiggle the nose, twitch it; take in a deep breath, then breathe out.

Mouth: Open the mouth wide; make different shapes with the lips; smile, pout, close up tight.

Tongue and voice: Wiggle the tongue, stick it out, try to touch the nose, then the chin; make sounds—clicking, humming, shouting, buzzing, growling, laughing, snoring, yawning, crying, cooing, singing.

The areas of problem solving and social awareness are especially important for the young child and show the need to compromise. After the individual exploration of separate parts of the body, the teacher can ask the children to choose a partner and make a head dance, an arm dance, a foot dance, or a hand

dance, or she can ask the children to dance
individually. The teacher may ask some children
to present their dance to the rest of the group.
After a few presentations, there may be a dis-
cussion—"What do you think of this dance?"
"Do you think that was a head dance?" "Did
they move together?" "Did they solve the
problem?"

LOCOMOTOR MOVEMENTS

Locomotion is going from one place to another
by

> walking
> skipping
> running
> galloping
> hopping
> crawling

or moving in any other way the teacher or the
child can suggest.

When first exploring locomotion, the teacher should encourage and emphasize large and free movements. Feeling the dynamic contrast of large and small in the muscles will stimulate interest in their movement, as well as teach the children—in another way—the concept of large and small. The same principle can be followed in the teaching of the concept of high and low.

The teacher can stimulate the children's moving by suggesting, "Feel big all over," and then contrast this with, "Feel tiny," urging them with her voice to be smaller and smaller. "Walk very high and very low. Now walk with your hands on the floor and turn over and walk with your stomach in the air. Try sitting down on the floor and move any way you can. Make up your own way of moving across the room on your stomach or on your back." The teacher should be performing these movements as she talks.

Hopping can be done singly, in combinations of two, three, or four, or with the whole class hopping together, on one foot, on both feet, hopping backward, forward, and sideward. This kind of movement helps to develop an awareness of direction and space.

The size and shape of the room will influence the size and shape of the movements the children will create. If the room has a very large area, more than likely very large and often running movements will result; the impulse is to fill up the space. The children will learn to adjust to smaller areas, and their movements can be just as satisfying.

Awareness of the rhythmic quality in motion is important. The accompaniment can be hand clapping, foot stamping, and such voice sounds as clicking, audible breathing, singing, and saying words—either single words or in combinations. Such sounds as groans and sighs may be the result of physical movement or may serve to stimulate action. Words themselves, whether real or made up, can be used effectively. Some improvised word sounds are so simple that many adults may experience difficulty in using them. But the children will enjoy the sound and rhythmic quality or even the words for their own sake, just as they find joy in movement for its own pleasure and not for a particular end result or intellectual purpose.

As a suggested activity, the teacher can say, as she walks, "Everyone walk around the room —without bumping into anyone else." This experience will stimulate awareness of the size and shape of the room; the problem is that of adjusting steps so as to move freely and comfortably by assessing the locations of the other people.

Or she can say, "Walk forward," "Walk backward," "Walk sideward," "Walk high," "Walk low," "Walk with giant steps," "Walk with tiny steps," "Walk heavy," "Walk light." The teacher's voice and actions should accent and express each new quality.

The teacher can ask for a new way of walking—"your own special way." She can then choose one walk that has a clear and unusual quality. She can ask the child to demonstrate

his walk in front of the whole group, and then everyone can do it together. If this walk has a very clear rhythmical beat, it can be emphasized by clapping hands, beating a drum, or stamping feet. The teacher should not change the quality of the child's work, only underline or clarify it.

For children who have not been accustomed to moving freely, walking, skipping, running, hopping, and crawling are excellent ways to introduce dance and to stimulate movement feelings concerning the pure pleasure of body motion, alone or in groups or in a line.

To make a line dance, the group should form a single line. With a drum or with hand clapping, the teacher or a child beats out a very simple rhythm (*1 2 3, 1 — 2 3,* or *1 2 — 3*). When the teacher feels the group has the beat, she can choose a leader who will lead the line all around the room in a snakelike movement, all moving freely (using arms and upper body, even turning) but keeping the line and the beat.

A line dance can be done with one child acting as the leader, creating his own movements with accented motions of the arms and legs. It should be simple, something easily seen by the rest of the line, *slow* at first, not changing the movement too rapidly so that it can be imitated and followed by the whole group, with everyone having a turn. The teacher should urge the child to do something new, something different, exploring all kinds of movements— high, low, sideward, forward, backward, loud, soft, fast, and slow.

SOUNDS

Sounds are all around us all the time. Learning to listen, to hear the different qualities of sound, is another area for exploration. The children have themselves, their hands and feet, their fingers and toes, their tongues and voices; all these and more can make the musical accompaniment to movement and dance. This kind of accompaniment is sound that comes out of movement.

The teacher should have the children listen to the sounds their bare feet make on the floor when they walk or run; each has a special rhythm and sound. Loud, stamping sounds or light, soft sounds can be made. When they swing their legs and their feet hit the floor, they will make a brushing or slapping sound. How about hopping, sliding, skipping, and jumping sounds? When the children are sitting on the floor still different movements and sounds will evolve. Hands, too—everyone knows they can clap, pound, and slap. Fingers can snap and the tongue can click. The children can make a great variety of sounds and rhythms depending on how much the teacher is willing to experiment. Clapping alternately long and short time patterns, and then moving the whole body to these rhythms helps to develop time concepts.

One dance activity using sound which is particularly oriented toward the individual is the name dance. Each child moves to the rhythm of his own name, sometimes accompanying the movement with clapping hands or stamping feet, while the rest of the children join in, moving and chanting the child's name. For example, a name such as Mary Jones will be heard as having three beats: *Ma ry Jones.*

$$\begin{array}{ccc} 1 & 2 & 3 \end{array}$$

Using the voice as an instrument brings to the dance experience one more part of the individual which can be involved. It is a beautiful accompaniment when everyone sings together—using the voices freely, making up songs—or just experimenting with sounds—

humming or wordless singing. The sounds and movements can develop together, holding a group together, helping them to have a common experience. It can be a good way to begin or to end a dance session. This particular kind of stimulus is also useful for language acquisition. The kinesthetic sense has tremendous potential for reinforcing learning processes, helping children with perceptual problems, and strengthening self image. Those with speech difficulties can benefit from exercising the tongue, the face, and the vocal cords. The teacher can experiment with the sounds *ah, oh, aw, eee, i,* and *uh!* By making the lips different shapes and exaggerating these sounds the children can have a wonderful time and can make up their own songs. It is an experience full of surprises and fun.

Laughing, crying, whispering, growling, snoring, buzzing, yawning, humming, roaring, shouting, cooing, purring sounds—all of these and any others that the teacher and the children can think of will evoke different movement and sound accompaniment. As the vocabulary grows both in language and in movement there will be opportunities to encourage and stimulate new dances, new words—and the teacher should not forget to try nonsense words just for the sound quality. This is a wonderful opportunity for humor, for everyone to laugh together. How about a laughing dance?

INSTRUMENTS

Instruments evoke movement and should be chosen on the basis of their durability and the sounds they produce. There must be enough instruments—at least one for each child—and if all of the children can have the same instrument, they can have an especially fine group experience. Instruments can include:

Rhythm sticks—these may be made from bamboo poles cut into six- to seven-inch lengths or rib bones acquired from the butcher, then cleaned and sanded.

Shakers—empty plastic bottles with beans inside and tops glued on.

Bells

Drums—have at least one that is large enough for several children to beat at once (large plastic wastebaskets or pans). Two-pound coffee cans, painted and with drum heads on both ends, can be made.

Tambourines

Cardboard tubes of different lengths

There is no end to the discovery of new instruments. Teachers and children can usually make their own, always searching for new sounds, shapes, and textures. Using the children's own rhythms, those arising from their feelings and movements, rather than imposing a musical mood or time pattern upon them, also increases their sense of acceptance, encourages their sense of worth.

Drums are especially rewarding and exciting. There are so many different kinds—African drums, large and small wastebaskets, tin and plastic, large coffee cans covered with skins, wooden drums made from big chopping bowls, a truck tire on which many children can beat at the same time. The drum beat can emphasize

the rhythmical feelings of the group or the individual. One child can play while the others move to his beat. Turns can be taken; this situation offers many opportunities for the child who beats out the rhythm for others to follow. He is aware that he is leading; he decides when the group will move and when it will stop. He

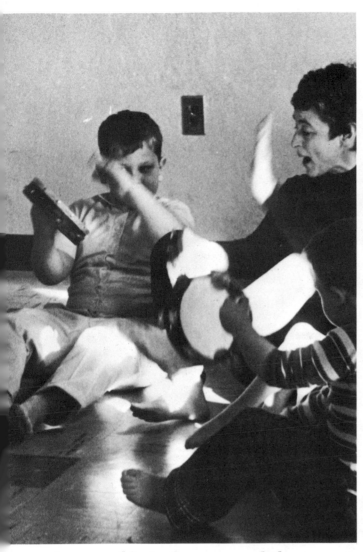

is responsible to the group and the group to him. When he does this with the teacher alone, he gets the unusual experience of equality on a level that rarely happens between a child and an adult. He also understands when the teacher beats the drum, and he follows. The nonverbal communication in this situation is dynamic and exciting.

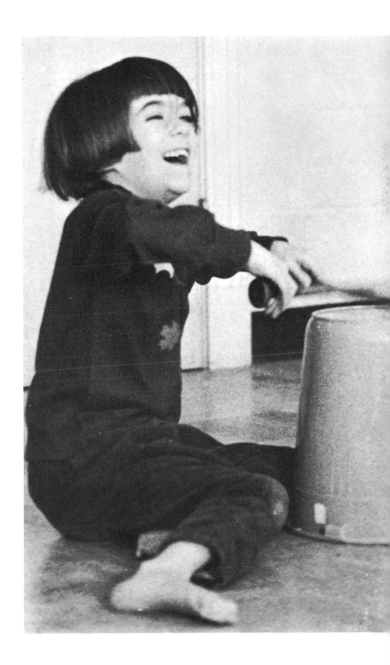

Bells provoke and stimulate new movements, not only for hands and wrists, but for feet and ankles. Rhythm sticks, rattles, tambourines, and shakers make different sounds when played by hand or tapped on the floor, door, and furniture.

Rhythm instruments are used to add another form of free expression to creative movement. The children are encouraged to use them as they wish, and, because they are not bound by conformity, they use them in ways that do not occur to adults.

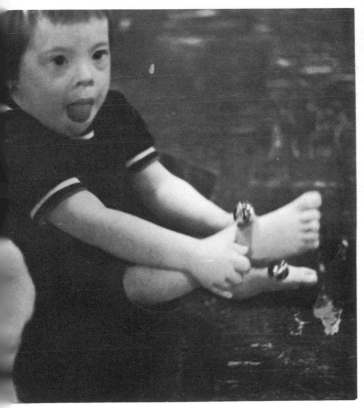

A circle dance can be tried by forming a circle
on the floor, with one child moving on the outside or inside (in his or her own way, walking,
running, skipping, jumping) and with the rest
of the group acting as an orchestra. The group
should wait until the child begins to move, to
hear and see what rhythmical quality his movement will have. Then the teacher, with the
children, can pick it up, moving to the beat
while sitting in the circle. The instruments the
children and teacher use can all be different
or all be the same—a variety of sounds can
be as exciting as the sound of fifteen or twenty
shakers being used as the orchestration.

REST TIME

Rest time will come naturally to the children. It will grow out of their need for quiet after so much activity. The rest period has traditionally had a scheduled time and can become a source of many disciplinary problems. But the rest period should come when it serves a need— stillness after so much motion, quiet after so many sounds, feeling no movement, hearing the silence.

It is important that the children discover in their bodies these different feelings of tension and relaxation, sound and silence, the polarity of activity and passivity. Recognition of these feelings can be an excellent aid in developing more self-awareness. And because children make their own accompaniment, their movements and sounds will ebb and flow. For each group has its own rhythm, as has each child in the group. The children determine the pace. The teacher is the guide, helping to create this balance between active and quiet experiences. This time is a creative pause for the children to replenish themselves.

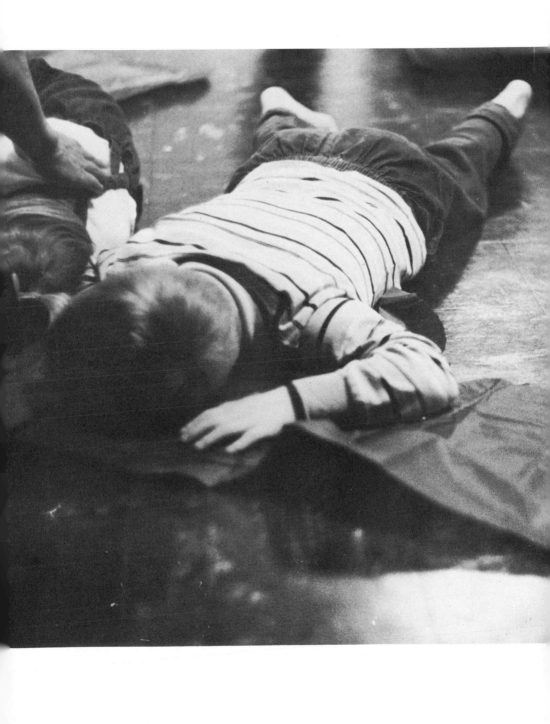

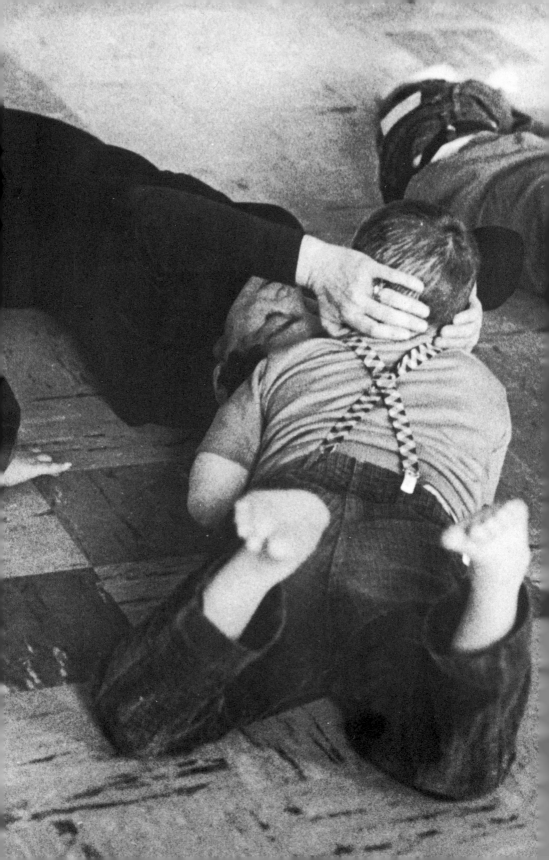

It is natural when a teacher and children dance together as a group that they rest together. So if one or two children show an inclination to stop and rest after a lot of activity, the teacher might suggest, "Oh, what a good idea! Let's all lie down and rest for a while." The floor is a perfect place to rest. It will hold everyone, lying softly and loosely. The teacher can talk about rest time, in a hushed whisper. "Shh, be still and listen to the quiet. It's so soft." If the teacher speaks, she should keep her voice very low, a musical accompaniment to the rest. Or the silence can be the music—just the sound of everyone's relaxed, quiet breathing.

Sometimes a child will rest his head or arm on another child who is lying close by. It is a warm feeling to rest near a friend. But there are times when it is good, even necessary, for the children to have their own places on the floor—a place where they are not touching anyone, where legs and arms can be flopped and bodies can be wiggled a bit before settling down, a place to yawn and stretch where there is no bumping.

The teacher should always rest with the children. Sometimes alone, sometimes in the middle of a group, sometimes touching a child, sometimes just looking at him, sharing the silence. This is a new and different relationship for the teacher and the child, on the floor together, feeling and seeing each other in another way. The teacher should not be in a chair, looking down, or at a desk working. There is no need of instructions for or demands from the child.

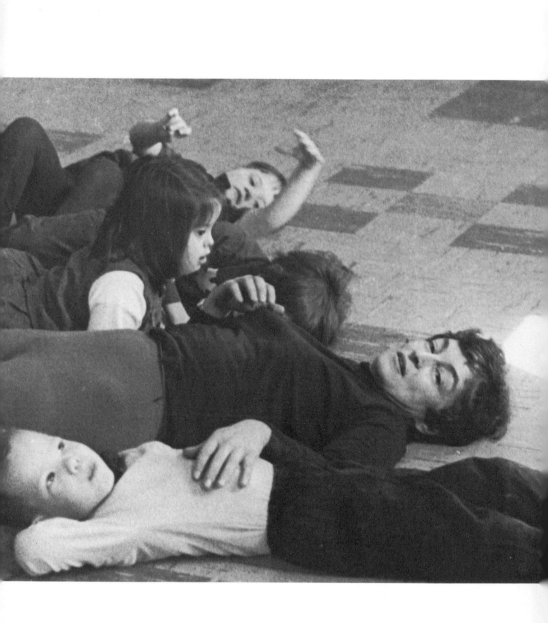

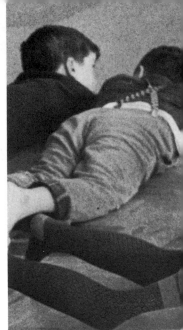

The children often rest with the materials and instruments they have used. Sometimes when two children have been sharing a large cloth, they will carefully spread it on the floor and lie on it together. They often wrap themselves in the materials with which they have been dancing. Sometimes they go to their cupboards to bring out their regular rest mats.

The rest time will continue until the children show, by getting up and starting to move about, that it is time to dance again.

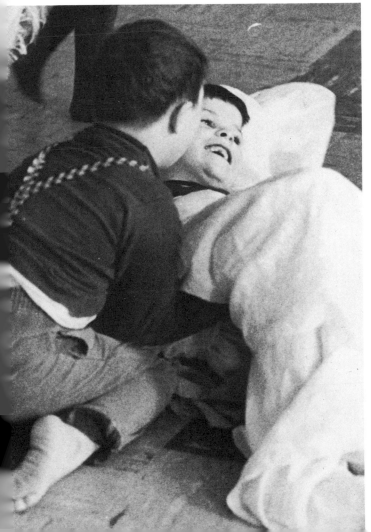

MATERIALS

Movement patterns change in relation to various kinds of materials used; they can be extended to enhance movements. Materials can bind people together; they can give one child a chance to be a leader, and another child an opportunity to be pulled along. Materials can be used to "draw in" the child who cannot reach out or relate with other people.

The variety of material which can be used is unlimited, depending on the ingenuity of the teacher and the children to discover all there is in the world to dance with and about. These are some of the materials:

> Tubular jersey cut into sections
> Parachute cloth
> Thick rope
> Elastic cord
> Colored tissue paper
> Cloths of different weights, colors,
>   and textures.

The way these materials are used is determined by each child. New textures and new shapes excite their sense of touch and stimulate perception. The atmosphere is set for experiment and discovery. When children feel the textures and shapes in relation to themselves, it helps them move out or away from their usual patterns of motion.

The involvement of the children grows as they become more facile and excited by their ability to work independently or with another child or children. This leaves the teacher free

to work with just one child who has been unable to dance, who might be more timid or less able to keep up with the other children. A large length of light cloth can be helpful in encouraging children to participate. Often it is the key which opens the door for such a child. It can also help children to dance together, to make an accommodation, giving and receiving.

This experience, in order to be successful, requires concentration and involvement—two factors in the learning and developing process. When this goes well the teacher can enlarge the problem-solving experience to trios and quartets—the need to compromise becomes even more evident and challenging.

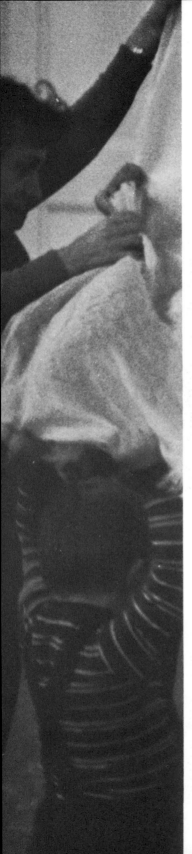

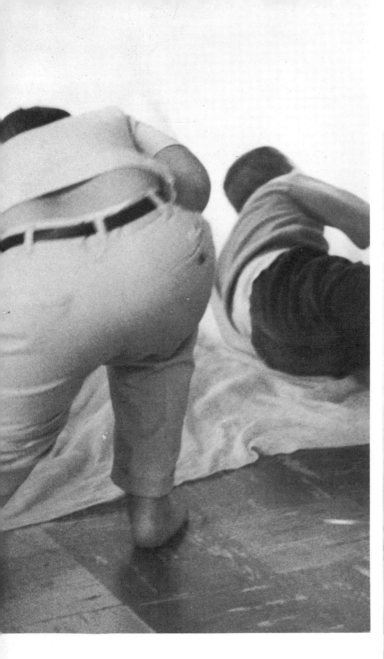

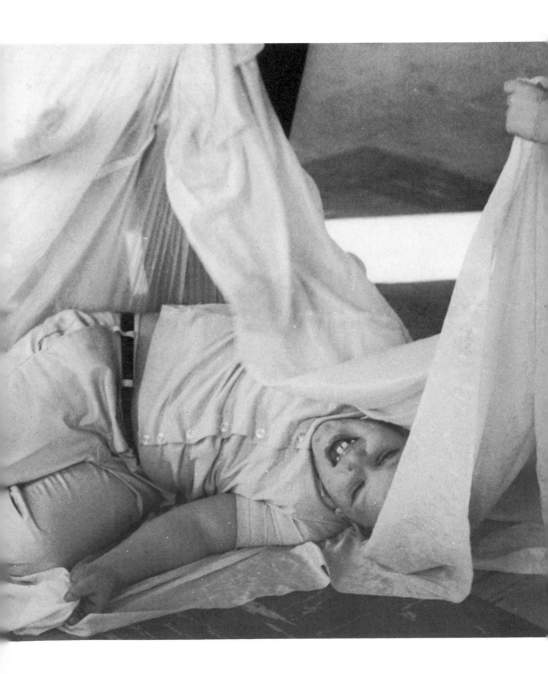

The teacher will find that cloth, tissue paper, elastic, and rope are best used toward the end of the class. Because these materials are relaxing and because the children are now warmed up physically and socially, they can work alone, in duets, or in larger groups. It is the time when the teacher can move from one child to another, perhaps staying a little longer with a child who needs more individual attention and who, because he or she receives it, will be able to work more successfully at the next session.

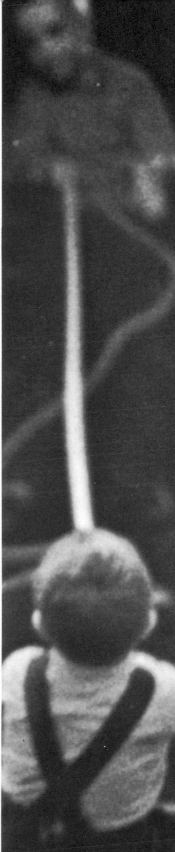

The dance period will usually grow from a twenty-minute session to an hour, depending on the regularity of the sessions and the creative leadership of the teacher.

If it is at all possible, the teacher should end with a group dance; and if it has been very exciting and stimulating the teacher and the children can all lie down on the floor for another rest. But very often the classes will end

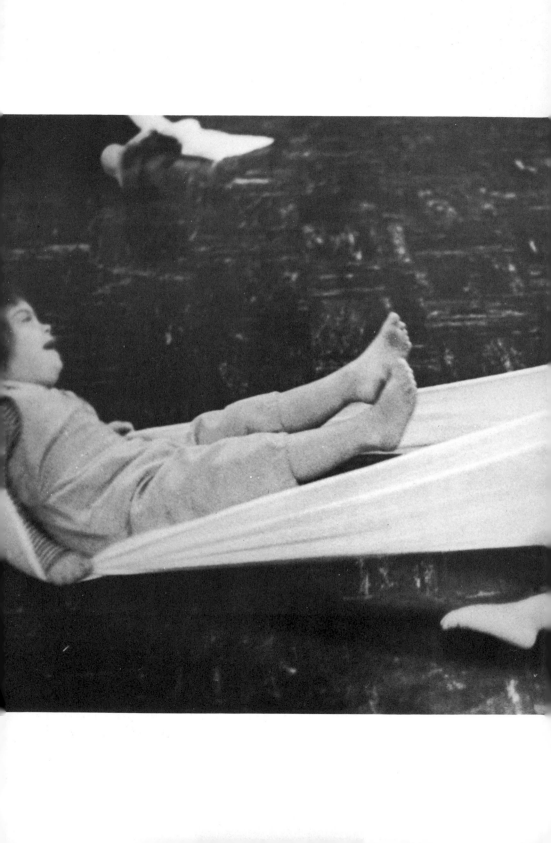

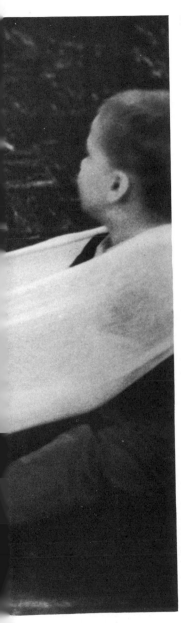

in an informal way, with the children working at their own tempo until someone puts his cloth away in the basket and starts to put on his shoes and socks. The teacher knows it is time to stop. There are times when an hour has gone by and there are two or three children still involved, making dances together or alone. Let it go on if possible, while the others who are finished can start getting ready for the next activity.

If the teacher will use the material and the creativity that exists in her and in her children, they will feel free from pressure and failure, and they will experience an exciting hour to dance alone or with each other as a group.

teachers' workshops

NOT EVERYONE feels and perceives movement to the same or even a similar degree. Some people are much more verbal, than movement oriented—especially in our present culture which educates the intellect far beyond our primitive and basic feelings of movement. It seemed only natural that the teachers, though not dancers themselves, become involved in movement exploration, in order to learn that exciting and rapid insights into the child could be gained through dance. Since it is up to the teacher to recognize and see with understanding eyes and feelings the dispositions and needs of her children, teachers' workshops are of great benefit in attaining this ability.

The excitement and involvement of teachers whenever they have participated in the workshops I have conducted have always kindled a fire in my mind and in my heart. They have supported me in their classrooms and talked to me about the children, their differences, and their problems. The teachers have helped me to learn and understand their needs and satisfactions.

A workshop can be conducted (with the necessary and opportune variations) like a classroom situation with the children. And, of course, a workshop is the place where practice in making simple instruments and other materials is best done.

When teachers participate and become involved in these dance workshops, which should meet at least once and sometimes twice a month, it is for most teachers more than just a time to dance; they enjoy the fun, the relaxation, and the creativity. The one- or two-hour period should be followed by discussions of situations which may have developed after using creative movement as part of the curriculum. It is a time for sharing and clarification of ideas and methods.

Each teacher has to learn to use the material in her own way; and although many teachers have a special time just for creative movement, they have put their learning to use in singing, finger painting, listening to music, and playing games indoors and out.

Technical skills are not necessary; a feeling for and enjoyment of movement, and a sense of fun, joy, and empathy are the minimum requirements. Because of this, there will be a measure of success for all who participate in a workshop.

With self-awareness comes awareness of others, and the potential which creative movement has in this area of development is perhaps its most exciting aspect and one from which all can benefit.

Bibliography

Bailyn, Bernard. *Faces of the Revolution*. New York: Knopf, 1990.

Bakeless, John. *Turncoats, Traitors, and Heroes*. Philadelphia: Lippincott, 1959.

Coburn, Frank. *The Battle of April 19, 1775*. Port Washington, N.Y.: Kennikat Press, 1912.

Fischer, David Hackett. *Paul Revere's Ride*. New York: Oxford University Press, 1994.

Gross, Robert. *The Minutemen and Their World*. New York: Hill & Wang, 1976.

Langgurth, A. J. *Patriots*. New York: Simon & Shuster, 1988.

Pearson, Michael. *Those Damned Rebels*. New York: Putnam's Sons, 1972.

Piper, Fred. *Lexington*. Lexington, Mass.: Lexington Historical Society, 1963.

Sabin, Douglas. *April 19, 1775: A Historiographic Study*. Concord, Mass.: National Park Service, 1987.

George III, the king who'd started his reign so well, ended badly. He passed his last years raving mad and chained to a chair.

The stubborn Yankees finally forced England to accept American independence in 1783. Thousands died in the American Revolution, including headstrong Major Pitcairn, who died at the Battle of Bunker Hill.

Disease killed Captain Parker months after the fight on the village green.

Samuel Adams and John Hancock signed the Declaration of Independence. Each was also later governor of Massachusetts.

General Heath continued to use book-learned war skills in the Revolution, as did the man who sold him the books, Henry Knox.

Paul Revere took part in several battles of the war. Later, he enlarged his reputation as a great silversmith.

Colonel Smith fought without distinction but still managed to be promoted to general.

Percy fought well but resigned his command in disgust with the war. He became the richest man in England.

General Gage lost the Battle of Bunker Hill and retired to England. In 1787, eleven years after America's Declaration of Independence, Gage died, still holding the title royal governor of Massachusetts.

The road between Charlestown and Concord lay strewn with dead men and horses. Seventy-three redcoats died and 174 were wounded. The Yankees suffered 49 dead and 39 wounded.

The fight of April 19 proved to be "a hinge . . . on which a large future was to turn." The battle, said writer Thomas Payne, set "the country . . . on fire above my ears."

Nearby lay the British warship *Somerset* and her roaring
cannons. As the sun set, the ship's guns frightened away
the Yankees. The regulars had finally reached safety.
Among the last to escape was Major Pitcairn,
a player in the very first fighting.

The British were nearly home, but the rebels had torn up the Charles River bridge that led to Boston, trapping the redcoats on the wrong bank. Cleverly, Percy abandoned the idea of reaching Boston and, instead, led his men to a hill in the waterside town of Charlestown.

Percy had once thought the Yankees were "villains" who "talk much and do little." Now he decided that they had "men amongst them who know very well what they're about."

The fighting continued into Menotomy, today's Arlington. Yankees and regulars fought from house to house.

Seventy-eight-year-old Samuel Whittemore hid himself behind a stone wall and attacked the redcoats with a musket, two pistols, and a sword. He killed one and wounded another before half his face was shot away, and he was bayoneted fourteen times. But "Flinty Whittemore" survived the ghastly wounds and lived until age ninety-six.

Forty regulars and twenty-five Yankees died in Menotomy.

He ringed the retreating British with militiamen and a circle of fire, and "helped . . . pull people together, advised the best use of terrain, moved units down on the British."

William Heath, a Massachusetts general, arrived to lead the Yankees. Heath was not a professional soldier but a country squire who'd learned war from books. He proved a close reader.

The wagons were ambushed by old men led by David Lamson, who killed the lead horses and two regulars and sent the rest of the redcoats fleeing for their lives. They surrendered at the soonest opportunity – which turned out to be to an elderly woman named Mother Batherick, who then delivered her prisoners to the local militia. Some in Britain later wondered, "If one old Yankee woman can take six grenadiers, how many soldiers will it require to conquer America?"

Skillfully using his cannons to keep the rebels at bay, Percy nonetheless worried he had too few cannonballs. Gage had had the same worry and had sent a small convoy with extra cannonballs after Percy. They never arrived.

A big-nosed, bony man from a family of great wealth and privilege, Percy was a cool leader. Using two cannons he'd dragged with him, he drove away the Yankees. Then he folded Smith's men in with his own, and prepared for a fight all the way back to Boston.

It was the work of newly arrived British artillerymen.

Back in Boston, a worried General Gage had dispatched Brigadier Lord Percy and another group of regulars with orders to assist Smith. Reaching Lexington in late afternoon, Percy was shocked to discover himself rescuing the colonel.

"Our ammunition began to fail, and [some] were so fatigued that they were scarce able to act," said a regular. "[It] made a great confusion. We began to run rather than retreat in order."

The militiamen, "maddened and beside themselves," followed the redcoats into Lexington. Utter British defeat was a whisker away.

Then "cannons began to play."

Militiaman Loammi Baldwin said, "A ball came through the Meeting House, near my head. I retreated . . . and lay and heard the balls in the air and saw them strike the ground."

The redcoats were ambushed again. This time, Major
Pitcairn was unhorsed. He was shaken but not wounded.
Five of his men weren't so lucky and were killed.

The regulars continued down the lane. As they retreated, the rebels "concluded to scatter and make use of the trees and walls for to defend us, and attack them." At a skirmish at a bend in the road that would be remembered as Bloody Curve, thirty redcoats fell. And outside Lexington, Captain Parker and his bloodied militiamen hid behind granite boulders and blasted the regulars at close range, knocking Colonel Smith from his horse with a thigh wound. The fight would be remembered as Parker's Revenge.

The redcoats started along the lane back toward Lexington. At Meriam's Corner, a crossroad along the redcoats' march, rebels formed a battle line. One joked, "Stand trim, boys, or the rascals will shoot your elbows off!"

The clash at Meriam's Corner left more than wounded elbows. "A great many lay dead and the road bloody," said Yankee Amos Barrett. Militiamen from twenty-three surrounding towns would eventually shed their blood in the battle.

Vast numbers of Yankees gathered in the hills as Colonel Smith assembled his men and ordered them back to Boston, twenty miles away. It was about noon. Many of the Yankees and British had been armed and on the move for ten hours and more.

"The weight of their fire was such that we was obliged to give way, then run," said British ensign Jeremy Lister.

Simple farmers, mechanics, and clerks had scattered the famed soldiers of the British army!

The regulars fled to Concord to join the main body of troops, the wounded hobbling after them. A local man, Ammi White, raced to an injured soldier on the road, splitting the redcoat's skull with a hatchet, to the horror of Yankees and British alike.

Finally, Major Buttrick of Concord yelled, "Fire, fellow soldiers, for God's sake fire!"

Muskets fired. Balls flew. Smoke billowed. Regulars fell: three dead and nine wounded.

Then, as at Lexington, a shot was fired. But this time there was no mystery. It came from a regular acting without orders. Two other redcoats joined in, then the entire front rank. Musket balls tore into the militia.

Isaac Davis, captain of the neighboring town of Acton's militia, fell dead, as did a comrade.

The young fifer and three others were wounded.

Still, the Yankees came on.

The colonel's old coat, flapped hat, and leather apron stood in shabby contrast to the splendid scarlet and gold uniforms of the British officers. Despite his unmilitary appearance, no one hesitated when the colonel ordered the men to load their weapons. He added the warning "not to fire until the British fired first."

A young fifer played a jaunty tune and they all went forward.

"They began to march . . . down upon us . . . in a very military manner," a regular remarked.

The militia's military bearing and larger numbers astonished the redcoats and they fell back.

In the town, Major Pitcairn led the search for powder and arms, discovering only a discouragingly small cache that included three cannons and wooden gun carriages. He disabled the guns and set the carriages afire. But as they burned, the flames leaped to the town's courthouse and it began to burn too. Despite their mutual distrust, the Yankees and redcoats joined together in a bucket brigade and doused the flames.

At North Bridge, volunteers swelled the militia's ranks until about five hundred were present. They saw smoke rise from Concord and feared the worst.

"Will you let them burn the town down?" one challenged militia colonel James Barrett.

About a hundred redcoats, a group splintered from the
main body, lined up against them on the other side of
the bridge.

At 9 a.m., the regulars reached Concord. At first, the militiamen withdrew from the town to a low hill beside the narrow Concord River. Below them was the North Bridge.

Smith allowed his men three victory cheers before ordering them to Concord. For most, it was the first time they learned of their mission.

They left the dead and the grieving of Lexington. But as the regulars marched the six miles to Concord, thousands of militiamen from surrounding towns rallied. The lanthorns Revere had shone hours earlier had set in motion alarm riders, signal shots, and beacon fires that had spread the call to arms everywhere.

Balls clipped part of
Lexington's Ebenezer
Munroe's earlocks, scraped his
clothes, and pierced his arm.
Militiaman Robert Munroe fell
dead where he stood.

Shot in the chest, Jonathan
Harrington crawled to his house at
the edge of the green and died on his own doorstep as his
wife and son watched.

Jonas Parker, a kinsman of the captain, fell wounded. On
the ground, he struggled to load his gun.

The Yankees fired back.

"All was confusion and distress," militiaman Joseph Seabrook
said.

Bullets flew. Men fell. The redcoats charged with bayonets
and killed Jonas Parker.

Colonel Smith arrived and discovered seven dead
militiamen, one dead regular, others wounded, and his men
acting less like soldiers than a mob. He forced them back into
disciplined ranks, saying, "I was desirous of putting a stop to
all further slaughter."

Their muskets spewed heavy leaden balls, belching so much smoke as they fired that clouds of it covered the green, hiding shooters and shot-at alike.

But the shot acted as a signal to the regulars who, without orders, fired first in ragged single shots, then in combined, roaring volleys.

Was it the British? The Yankees?
The answer remains a mystery.

Captain Parker told his men, "Stand your ground! Don't fire unless fired upon! But if they want to have a war, let it begin here."

"Huzza! Huzza! Huzza!" yelled the regulars and formed a battle line.

Onlookers gathered at the edges of the green.

From horseback, Pitcairn shouted, "Throw down your arms, ye villains, ye rebels!"

Greatly outnumbered, Parker probably recognized the folly of resisting. He ordered his men to "disperse and not fire," and most of them turned away. None dropped their weapons.

A shot!

"Some of the rebels who had jumped over a wall fired," Pitcairn said.

"Some of the villains [who] got over the hedge fired at us," said another British officer.

It came from "the corner of a large house," other soldiers claimed.

Militiaman Thomas Fessenden said an officer next to Pitcairn "fired a pistol."

Minister Clarke also claimed one of Pitcairn's officers "fired a pistol towards the militia as they were dispersing."

"If I draw my sword but half out of its scabbard, the whole banditti of Massachusetts will run away," he once bragged.

Now, on the Lexington Green, two lines of the so-called banditti stood before him.

Dawn and the redcoats arrived together. At the head of
their march was Major John Pitcairn, leading about 240 men.

As they left, the Lexington militia mustered. Fifty to seventy men raced to join John Parker, their captain and a veteran of the earlier French and Indian Wars. A farmer and mechanic, Parker was forty-six and dying of tuberculosis. His men ignored his ill health and unflinchingly followed him onto the grassy field at the town's center.

Windows flew open and, like turtles emerging from their shells, sleepy heads popped out, including Adams's and Hancock's.

The men believed that Gage's main mission was to seize and destroy the colonists' gunpowder at Concord. Revere, accompanied by rider William Dawes, was sent on to Concord with a warning while Hancock and Adams made their escape from Minister Clarke's house.

After a rowboat took Revere to Cambridge, he mounted a mare named Brown Beauty and raced off. The moon was bright. He rode hard for an hour, dodging British patrols, until he reached the Clarke house at midnight. Revere banged on the door.

On their heels was the determined Paul Revere. He feared the redcoats meant to march to Lexington and capture Samuel Adams and John Hancock, leaders of the colonial opposition who were staying at Minister Jonas Clarke's home there.

Only their officers knew where they were going or what was expected of them. Each soldier carried a day's provisions and thirty-six rounds of powder and ball for their muskets.

At 2 a.m. they started forward, tramping one square-toed boot in front of the other.

Meanwhile, on the Boston waterfront, Colonel Francis Smith led nearly nine hundred British infantrymen, grenadiers, and royal marines onto longboats. They dutifully stood closely packed as sailors rowed them across the Back Bay to Cambridge. They waded ashore at a marshy beach, soaking themselves up to their waists. The night was cool and the men shivered inside their linen britches and red woolen coats.

He sent John Pulling and Robert Newman to the old
North Church with two "lanthorns," lanterns fashioned with
paper-thin slices of cow horn in place of glass. They climbed
to the top of the church's steeple, lit the lanthorns, and held
them out a window.

The twinkling lights were a message for Revere's allies
outside of Boston.

"If the British were out by water we would show two
lanthorns . . . and if by land, one."

The two lights sent news spreading throughout nearby
towns: Beware — soldiers were coming quickly by boat!

Afterward, silversmith Paul Revere and others opposing the king vowed not to be surprised again by General Gage. Revere, square jawed and steady eyed, organized a Committee of Observers, lookouts on watch for another powder raid by the "regulars," as the British soldiers were known.

On April 18, 1775, a spy brought news to Revere and his friends that Gage's soldiers were preparing to march again. Revere had already concocted a plan to spread the word.

News of the powder "robbery" unleashed terrible anger and sent thousands of furious Yankees into the streets. The mob fell upon hated Tories, Americans who sympathized with the king, and threatened them, smashed their property, and chased them from their homes.

Meanwhile, General Gage made his first move to disarm
the colonists. In the early hours of September 1, 1774, his troops
sneaked from their Boston barracks to a powder house in
nearby Middlesex County, the largest supply of gunpowder in
Massachusetts. There, they grabbed 250 half barrels and returned
home before the outfoxed colonists awakened to the seizure.

Gage decided to separate the colonists
from the weapons and gunpowder with which
they could make mayhem. To carry out his plan,
he picked the home of the most quarrelsome colonists:
Boston, Massachusetts.

General Gage thought the Bostonians to be the "greatest
bullies." In 1773, Bostonians had dumped crates of tea in the
harbor rather than pay tax on it. The Boston Tea Party cheered
the Yankees, but left the king considerably less amused. He shut
down the harbor, crippling business and punishing the
Bostonians. But the king's attempt to enforce
the obedience of his colonists backfired.
Opposition to King George's rule drew
the colonists together in opposition.
In September 1774, representatives of the
American colonies gathered for the First
Continental Congress in Philadelphia.

It was tough talk, but the general, a sober-faced man used to making weighty decisions, was torn. America had been his home for nearly twenty years. He'd acquired property and wed a beautiful New Jersey heiress. "Bloody crisis" had to be avoided. But how?

By 1775, both sides were prepared for war. The time for "conciliation, moderation, and reasoning is over. Nothing can be done but by forcible means," said General Thomas Gage, the British military commander in America.

Dismayed at first, the Americans soon grew angry, then riotous. Violence flared. Britain answered with harder, stricter laws. Warm feelings that had existed for generations between Britain and her American colonies chilled.

In 1763, England's young King George III, only twenty-six years old, had found himself the victor of the Seven Years' War. Britain had defeated the French, Austrians, and Spanish and had won colonies around the world. Celebration was surely in order.

But George III could not celebrate.

Victory had not come cheap. Britain bowed under a huge war debt and the expense of governing an enlarged, far-flung empire. Something had to be done.

The king and his ministers cast about for a solution, and their eyes fell on Britain's American colonies. Convinced that the Americans were not contributing their fair share to the mother country, King George and his advisers decided to lighten the burden on the empire by lightening the pocketbooks of the Americans. New taxes — on cloth, sugar, almanacs, newspapers, and tea, to name a few — were levied on the American colonies.

April 19, 1775

A strong brown mare carried a messenger through a moonlit night to a simple house on a country lane. The messenger banged on the door. Windows flew open and, like turtles emerging from their shells, sleepy heads popped out to discover the source of the commotion.

It was vital news the messenger brought. News, it might be said, that took twelve years to arrive.

To Mindy and Lloyd

Published by Flash Point, an imprint of Roaring Brook Press

Roaring Brook Press is a division of Holtzbrinck Publishing Holdings Limited Partnership

175 Fifth Avenue, New York, New York 10010

www.roaringbrookpress.com

Distributed in Canada by H. B. Fenn and Company Ltd.

Library of Congress Cataloging-in-Publication Data

Brown, Don, 1949-

Let it begin here! : April 19, 1775, the day the American Revolution began / Don Brown. — 1st ed.

p. cm.

ISBN-13: 978-1-59643-221-5   ISBN-10: 1-59643-221-7

1. Lexington, Battle of, Lexington, Mass., 1775–Juvenile literature. 2. Concord, Battle of, Concord, Mass.,

1775–Juvenile literature. I. Title.

E241.L6B77 2008   973.3'311–dc22   2008011221

Roaring Brook Press books are available for special promotions and premiums.

For details contact: Director of Special Markets, Holtzbrinck Publishers.

First Edition December 2008

Book design by Jennifer Browne

Printed in China

2   4   6   8   10   9   7   5   3   1

April 19, 1775:

The Day the American Revolution Began

LET IT BEGIN HERE!

DON BROWN

ROARING BROOK PRESS

NEW YORK

LET IT BEGIN HERE!